CUT SIDE DOWN

JESSI MACEACHERN

INVISIBLE PUBLISHING
Halifax | Fredericton | Picton

Library and Archives Canada Cataloguing in Publication

Title: Cut side down / Jessi MacEachern.
Names: MacEachern, Jessi, 1988- author.
Identifiers: Canadiana 20240501748 | ISBN 9781778430596 (softcover)
Subjects: LCGFT: Poetry.
Classification: LCC PS8625.E23 C88 2025 | DDC C811/.6—dc23

Edited by Julie Joosten
Cover design by Megan Fildes
Interior design by Megan Fildes | Typeset in Laurentian
With thanks to type designer Rod McDonald

Invisible Publishing is committed to protecting our natural environment. As part of our efforts, both the cover and interior of this book are printed on acid-free 100% post-consumer recycled fibres.

Printed and bound in Canada.

Invisible Publishing | Halifax, Fredericton, & Picton
www.invisiblepublishing.com

Published with the generous assistance of the Canada Council for the Arts, the Ontario Arts Council, and the Government of Canada.

For Nana
who led me into the water.

For Hughie
who held the book & said "I get it."

RAVISHING THE SEX INTO THE HOLD

DO I ENJOY THE WORK?

Start here with the cut edges of the book.
They are standing at attention for you.

A light bulb or several hang in silence.
Hang so they're luminescent. It's plain
in my slovenly body on flesh-saturated
sheets —
        there are women wearing
ruffled underpants just behind my eyes.
I refuse their charms. I blink steadily
to pursue their invitation inside
        the mind. Their watches stop
my weakened experience
of time. Waves undo
the body
                'RS torrid choreography.
Excuse the lapse   in protocol.
My body doesn't belong
                                here,
late at night. One florid goose crows inside
a black sulphur storm. By morning
the women behind my eyes will all
be life-sized. They reveal the damage done
to the surface of worlds.

RAVISHING THE SEX INTO THE HOLD

The Eighteenth Century Is Silent

My inkpot finally ceased blushing.
With the heavenly hierarchy
I dipped my pen.
I told my fellow poets we were only the bodies
of ghosts following birds of the heart.

My evergreen rioted & the room
dropped to pieces. By the time
the men looked up from their scrub
the garden could be mistaken for women's cheeks.

In the eighteenth century I could try prose. Women
were ambling off
& the yellow-slashed sky
with roseate hue

had something no one felt. Denial was the difference
where the men now encouraged us
to write without dismay

over the climate. Feather after feather slashed
into every shrubbery.
How very few hallow'd words there now are.

I could scarcely keep the heart working.
What d'you call a shrubbery sea-stained, blood-soaked?

The Twenty-First Century Invents Sound

I plucked the orange
foam earplugs
from the goddess' ears. His mouths formed
their insensate black hole & I caught the reverberations
on my bare breasts. The screen of my chest
flickered
& the mountains became a neatly tattooed x.

The holy trinity was now a polycule. Its edges
careened into profanity. I mean, the ass on her!
It feels necessary to pause & ask for forgiveness
in the open marriage of the heart. My pussy

is leading the charge. Divine tragedy
is uproariously funny to me.
The many bodies are now one ruin
but I know ruins do not exist.

Who will honour my nightly fantasy of escaping
this flesh & entering the city like an odour

permeating the lusty thoughts of old dogs & rose gardens.
Who will hear that I speak the truth
when I say I am no one

& have never been?

One Sweet Will Agitate a Thousand

Already trouble enough our whole posse took
small doses daily.
My crumpled silk sheltered a fine gentleman
who would willingly
run with blood. Servants' asses eased his heart.

I bred glow-worms. Agony made evident some
bad accident.
We took contortions & subtleties to the window-
seat under the miasma.

I talked hither & thither of solitude.
O, life, documents, both,
butcher the poet,

so these lines are short of the necessary conceits
but above all you should know this: poetry was dead.
O, the poet uttered protestations. Time passed & our elephant
-footed deity swelled. I asked, What is love but time
in the mouth of the moon-god
consenting to be bound & gagged,

                                        honey

on the nipple of the sun-soaked warrior
recently slain,

                                        anguish

pouring like so many waves
over the lost city?

My dahlia grew thick. When the feasting finished
I was abundance: thorned & intricate. Curiously
put together,
I was full of vermin.

Eyes Were Always Short Cuts Known

A damask rose catches my foot.
In its own cupidity, greetings, jests
& bowl of darkness the rose
came on me pinching.

Hearing the guns confessing their sins
                                        I rose &
                                        I sank four more times.

Do I rhapsodize the simple architecture
                                        warmth &
                                        merriment?
My sighs were raindrops eddying & swirling upon
                                        the piers &
                                        pillars of one man's sex.
I instantly coloured red. Gradually
the flutter seemed fresher.

In perfect French, kissing a girl, I felt the pulse of youth
& the sun sink. Beyond the crowd, windows were hung
with yellow. Another tongue made in me such a welter up
& down.

The Princess plus belle que l'autre. In me were provoked
                                        such blushes
                                        transformation
took place. Half-conscious air, no English
blood, bowl of rose,
                                        on the ground &
                                        then such a howl

in my ears. I gnawed it, eager to come.
Quicker & quicker,
this man came opposite

& into the hold.

Bone Was Inferior to Them

To look more ravishing, I trod the grape
& changed sex. This was my blast.

I admit to some slight haziness nearest whatever
was worn indifferently by queens & ladies.

Love, a disease, more of foreigners, will yet endure. I went
on as she. As he, I almost threw

myself at any willing disposition. As she, I was told
his God prefers a sunset

to a million martyrs. Both were negligible. My natural
charms shattered & hiding in my mother's bosom.

I am some lad or his maiden on some hilltop,
young, noble, beautiful.

A curious fact, as he, alone, she was enough.

A Lover Could Remain Both

I could not help but rise. My companions became notorious

sculptors being slowly opened

by the teeth. My knees flushed. Every rose

-poor bush was apostrophizing the usual divinities.

Every market florist knew how the future aged the critics.

I required the teeth

of these cracked husbands. With cheeks like a wave, I became

a besotted cheerleader as bricklayers do.

When night came, a myriad stars gazed & gazed on me

who twisted. I became

the bounty when night came with its pen so quick to stir

a ripple & curve. Beast &

flood decorated the room all bearded gods desire

is night.

Stoop to His Bootstrap Buckles

In the illumination of my many eyes,
the Lord fulfilled his most amorous lady. I
was the poor foolish fellow in high feather. I
was suddenly & violently fulfilled.
My wine was double faced.

I fastened thought to spring & followed winter.
Something of fascination,
memories of burrowing into piled furs
to be smothered alive.

The exact opposite.

I was nude underneath the intricate justaucorps' brocade
the blue surtouts like a modest effort
to become the azure sky. My frill
was its own live thing, stopping the breath

so pleasurably.

Sailing ships were unable to follow me. I drew
the curtain &
stooped to fasten this thought where peaches ripen.

He was giving birth cold as ice. I caught the body
's genuflecting riot. She made the faculty of speech so free
love began
with mirrors:

I have two faces
or more
jostling each other
in Desire's bustling skirts.

Dimly Victorian & Woolgathering

Some spirit plunged my pen in hollow writing. I
complained of time & the rose bushes
thought nothing whatsoever.

My gout might perform another profound bow.
But what about my husband?

I was delivered of innumerable volumes. My first
child, the eighteenth century,
delivered me.

I thought my reverence for print excessively interesting.
Several park keepers
in impossibly tight scarlet trousers thought
my elegance useless.

The spirit of the century passed & my biographer plunged
her pen into my gowns
& flowers. The fashionable world knew
my testicular manuscripts

were only a dumb show. Innumerable little shops provided
my way to wealth
& power. Wealth & power did not exist.

I was my naked lord now risen
& incalculable after April came bank to bank thinking

he came so my conclusion might be conveyed
on the brink & she came beneath
beneath my lips.

I now beheld in our pushing a little elegance. To squeeze it
now struck up fervent desire. As no lady, I held
the barrel-shaped organ. The husband is going up & up.
The husband is a tribute in one's mind.

How Sex Swayed & Was Nothing

Showing timidity, both my cheeks
availed their plumpness against how royalty was dead
or ready to die. Here I nodded &
even my bones leant out the yellow coach
as a woman I loved sound as a man
I was no nice judge as a lover.
The blowing leaves stripped my satin-coloured scarlet.
The blowing leaves were asserting their right to ascend
were a lover's hands free to hurt.

A love-drunk hallucination asks me to tea
a book's gutter is one place for the thumb.

I was a well-favoured Lord
an overheated dancer with the impetuosity of the diseased.
I could not control the mania of my limbs
with the Law's permission I disassembled the organs
compulsively. Fungus overwhelmed the passionate brains
held in our tight trousers & voluminous skirts.

Timidity slipped in the dance

& I was boldly

living death.

Where the Waves Wear the Yellow

Women wore the sacred responsibilities,
the flowered paduasoy. The buzzing koalas saved
the looking glasses only to keep them
covered. If I am to save my queenly demeanour
I must uphold the greatest decorum. If the gift
was a lily, I promised to draw him closer to my bosom.
The closer we drew the more like a lily was mine
& his. Stray dog or pool of pus,
I would return in peau de soie.
This is a very complicated kind of love.

Men abandoned their spears for finer points
masterful weavers after all. The pythons tasted
morning's first spurts & asked for more. No
language can contain their convulsions. Words
— *sex, garments, death* — turn to ash in the mouth.
But we thrill in the deceit!

I reek of garbage & my head is shaped like yellow.
The weather is decked out
in padesway. I am a bumboat woman
taking her coffee like a thousand others. I have it!
I am a score of blue, a poet's forehead, an army
of young fellows ravishing the opinion.
D'you take sugar? inquired the women in Padua. Say,
young fellows, leave
the pinochle players alone. Biological certainty,
a thought fools cut into dark garments. Restraining
my tongue in the ardour between bank to bank. Now
am I woman?
As a man, a rapid notion up my skirts.
The chalky cliffs murmur,
How delightful!

Evening's Predatory Landing

If I appeared petulant throwing my book
down in the spotless square so that its spine bristled
& its pages formed an haute couture skirt
so be it.   I was alone in a glimmer
meant to be a place for planning the future.
If emptiness & nothingness cannot be taken
                                        at their word
take the word of the birds overhead, for these
reptiles are having the time
of their lives
swooping low over the pristine sidewalks
          loitering against the silent mailboxes
          preening their tailfeathers in a direct affront
to me
the creator of this heap of bird shit.   Understand
this is what moved me to the precipice
of the mountaintop on which I stand
overlooking the empty city.   I visited
hotels, ordered glasses
of prosecco, pretended loyalty
to a team, asked,
          "Randolph?"
in response to the guttural introduction
of many moustached fathers; the hotels
were not cheap
but someone else was always paying, the alcohol
mysteriously slow to take effect,
the fervour with which a goal was celebrated
                                        deafening,

& each papa's moustache curiously waxed
into three rising spires.   The city
was not mine, but it made me
the quandary I am: stranger
& citizen.   The commons
is nothing & I am without
a population from whom to be estranged.
Alone
I shield my beehive
from the bird
shit pellets raining from the sky.
There are never
                                                  any ruins
for the city as I remember it never existed;
all is dust. We are at the beginning.

Living is a Cold Clarity

Having grown preoccupied with death
    & biography
        here I am in another tongue
Transporting into the gloom
    the voluptuousness
        of my indulgent childhood

History reflects
    my wildness
        History is
a testament of my foolish & impossible
        imagination
Part snow, cream, cherries
    & furs
        sex

Sneering at them
    won't change the fact
        of my velvet manners
end the passionate doubt
    of my biography's unfinished
cherries, muffs, opulence

I am looking over Savage Harbour
at an age for wearing pearls

It is my mother's scarlet blood you blame
for the coldness
Clarity is something
hidden

Inviting the intellect to water's fall
you alone light flame
to reason & plunge us
into the ambrosial overflow.

A Lover Could Not Name Language

Men of genius came over me. Other people said,
finally, nothing. My several accusations
against the page remained. I was a foolish wretch
waiting for the reluctant escorts to pour the tea. Truth beat
upon my every part. Now, the swans are alone. Now,
women are the architecture. Whatever
their occupation, their lotus collars are but monstrous
growths. I take my white levity
through the sky. As a skilled housekeeper
I peer & grope
the small company assembled in the mall.
I've heard nothing, I said. I've heard
nothing. Both dubious guardians
stopped pouring out tea. Being somewhat deaf,
I said,
I've heard nothing.
My illusion revived. A moment
in utter darkness cut their gentle throats.
My red aces were constantly alight, so very bright.
My Kitty Rose opened. In utter darkness or joy
ladies may fidget.
Kitty Rose taught me this.

In the Hollow Writing & Thinking

I hold in this space the wedding ring
sullen & foreign looking, long in coming

The deep sigh fluttering through a whole year
slipping out of the telegraph wires

The fountains falling over the tomato-soaked pages
the royalties arrived

I am any rose awaiting the kingfisher
talking nonsense & prayer

Denial tries to come

like a precocious child Love's slipping
upon the spirit

Human beings alone
never felt better

I recite the calendar
in order to read all the world
The summer morning's hind legs grew

into sleek, splendid objects marked
by meadow-sweat
& life, in a flash,

permitted a very superstitious reverence for spider-thin boats
& the precise blood of dreams

Magic Show

I was in the bedroom at last! That vast erection still peering
in the moonlight. At a touch,
the thumb led me in. At a touch something else hung.
                    I was struck.
A person's life is an open invitation to desecration. I held these
words when seeking
pretty & ambitious girls. I knew the body's sorrows
            & joys.
Like a shell my mother's
absence unfurls here. Her shadow was shocked
by the red velvet
opera house. Children ran
out of my mind.
            Their hands
clasped a green screen.   The visible world was
a dog's ear twitching.
Needing another set of vows, the garden blowing, I stood naked.
Nothing moved between my selves & the light.

Through the garden into my mind privacy was called away.
                    People buzzed
& croaked in the shell's ears. Magic returned.
I was no longer a fruitful hunting ground,
though   I looked innocent as a clown   powdering
myself into pat resolutions.
Let the reader have the good humour to slow down.
Elsewhere, it was already blazing noon
& I had all but forgotten
the shock of time.

My mother looked into the face of her changeable son
& spat.
            I was wet,
so the thing to do was open the pages
& thrust my stiffness into the dark.
Achilles was weeping
in a macramé tunic weaved by Penelope.
            To possess
            a limb
            is to want
            another.

Fancy's Gone Off Her Head

Flinging my inheritance to the memory of ground
& recoiling from the difficult music
of its descent, I took flight. This was possible
while the old species' finale was being constructed.
Suddenly the gleaming midnight star, I was the sign
& symbol to which womankind drank
& prayed. Divine, eternal, iron-clad, I was
a constellation like no other;
the squirming fanatics forgot themselves
& their reproductive inventions in the bird-dotted landscape
& bared their breasts to my empty promises.

I was star-falling & in my foolishness
& somnambulism so vulnerable
to the grand dismissal. Mankind had taken
into custody the wind & was rapidly
set on inventing a new & airy species.
Of course no such venture could be without
an avalanche of complaint. I considered
the glaring possibility that our window for survival
had closed; knowing my individual plight
was of infinitesimal importance & gaining the advantage
of laughter, which streamed from my lips
like pear-shaped satin, I was in a thrall to the new
designer species being proposed. Never achieving
a countenance sturdier than misled
mothers-in-law or fire-haired entrepreneurs, their literate
bodies would make gluttony a virtue.

A Role in the Executive

In public I speak about the importance of care
& community. In private
I close my legs & stop the birth of desire.
I am more than these two
quagmires. I am also in the shadow's crowd
touching myself underneath the red
-checkered tablecloth. In History's well-appointed
lavatory shaving my breasts.

In the hotel of my adolescence I spoke to a corpse
whose green lungs taught me
to drink deeply from the ocean's barrel. I stole
the coins left for the boatman
& paid my toll off the island. Groping my way

into the new world, I became a small & able
atom of deceit. While searching
for your latest book

in the roaring agora, I took the question
of a fortune teller who
revealed an incestuous plot. I am wrong about this.
I was being scolded by a saintly hoard.

Alone & nude in the fetid harmony
of my several shames I asked for more.
She came blue
& about to cast the lure.

To Make Risotto You Must Suffer

I would like a man to measure my hips
& determine them perfect for child-bearing. I
would like a woman to take me

into her mouth & bite off the excess. I
would like a throng of unethical monogamists

for my playthings. Midnight
is lasting longer
& the witching hour

grows hungrier. I tattoo your last words
into my left thigh
by heating the needle
& rolling in the ink. The mess

is perfect. You spoke no language
I understood.

I am beginning to collect new streams
of income. Our liquor cabinet
is a gaping wound.

I like to throw my entire face
into its obliterative vacuum.

With enough time & enough fraud, I will
have the nation's largest collection of yellow chartreuse.

This is for the purposes of making the bartenders pant.
You are panting in rocky anticipation
for I am corseted

& threatening to turn the switch.
In mutual envy we turn to face the other's lover.

Cunt Was Her Favourite Word

I was open to it

& changed by it.

I was sitting pretty

in a private bed

& waiting to be made a spectacle. Dying
to have my sides split & insides prodded.
I hoped to lose count of the white jackets
in the room of my transformation.

Since this is fantasy I can say
the room was my mind
the bed your sweetly smiling face.

In fourteen centuries I've had one lover
with whom I copulate rarely but ferociously.
We are so ill made for each other
that the love-making causes harm.

I walk gingerly into the conversation
about pursuing another's genitals. Would a new bush
be the spice we need? Would some young
crowing take us into another century?

You back down History's halls
& wield a femur bone in response. We will
proceed as two
or more

giantesses.
Absence is no thing
to mourn. It feeds
our immortality.

The Nose Drove Me Mad

I went into the garden & discovered death had fled. Every petal
animatedly alive. It was my own design. Understand
I do not know who I've become. I stood like the mast
of a moored ship & centuries passed.

The ocean dried. I descended into dirt.
          You were already rolling in it.
          I was already inside your cavernous mouth.

Do you love my womanhood? Do you love the weird little guy
I've become? Do you love
                              the body lean & hard
                              the mind circuitous?
Now I am the flatulence hanging in the empty room.
Our modernist masters like it, so we do too.
Now I am the raised edges of paper
                                        made wet
                                        the body
                                        pressing into it.
Such a stench as this makes me blush. You dip
your fat thumb into the red
& discover my secret
delicacy. See how fast

I change fidelities: pursuing now death, now life,

                                                  now sex
                                                  garments
                                                  desecration.
Our palms make black imprints in the meat
of my childhood's thighs
                                                the pungent earth
                                                a flagging quality
of crisis. To return to the garden, I get on all fours
                                                & howl.
                                                We are all barking
into the future.

DO I ENJOY THE WORK?

I Belong to the Women

I am reading a book on architecture.
Everyone I know is reading the same woman
and her linguistic blocks. I imagine everyone
I don't know similarly reading
the woman's ephemeral commons.
I begin talking to the book.

A woman talking to a book is an everyday thing
in that it is in danger of being branded personal.

The future comes ambling back. A woman has
no special status. We are all feeling subjects.

I address the book as Renee.
I am speaking to the writing as it
scaffolds the page.
I am speaking back to what hails me.
"Hello," says the sudden voice of a man.
"Hello," says Renee (the book).
Hello.

Playing with ventriloquism is pulling at the threads
of the party banner. Still, there is the utopian ideal of laughter

uncoerced. A woman talking to a book is an everyday image
captioned "Blown back by history."

It is true that I am reading *Event Factory*
like everyone I know and everyone I don't.
But I cannot have my hands
in one taffeta confectionery at a time.

There are also the red crenulations
of Woolf's *Orlando*
and the sour cherry jam pots
of Niedecker's *Collected Works*.

A woman is reading a book in the middle of traffic.
Mindfulness leaves the public open to more than a paper cut.

The body is vulnerable to losing its visibility. Dar is a name
to which a woman attaches the smell of a body in mourning.

A woman takes a dose of allegory to time travel.
It is the present she would like to encounter.

The present is two stick figures embroiled in
a shootout captioned "We had a map we didn't use."

A name is simply a public body
on the street and the fact of traffic halted
workday interrupted profit flagging
citizen faces red citizen faces transported.
A name is a feeling adrift on the banners
abandoned roadside and caught in the wind.
There is a word for this bawdy mess
and the political desire
for an unending caress.

A ceramic blue plate contains
what is necessary.
In the mouth is a lamentation.
There is a word
for the embarrassment of too-little.
It catapults into view and loses its head.

Virginia and Lorine
refuse to leave me alone with the joy of the man's voice.
They are poor moral compasses
but they know he belongs to that other textual edifice
and, if he should slip into my mind,
they want to see the bulge
in the forehead, the cerebral hemorrhage.

Renee slides underneath the bookcase.
I am on the floor
making myself into a spectacle,
contorting my body to grow closer to the book.

A woman placed her book on the blue ceramic plate
so the primary word became "Crumb."

This is the danger-signal for the father. His preferred daughter
makes a gift of gardenias. They never arrive. This satisfies.

Lorine shines my desk lamp on the far wall
and creates a shadow play in which
modernist writers go on living. Virginia
is ruining the whole thing
by pacing back and forth
in the path of the light. But her wide yawns
are welcome punctuation in the silence
and, after all, Lorine doesn't seem to mind

the added constraint
of another textual body.
Its declarative science is not mine
but I plucked joy (named Simon) from its gestural rituals.
I must now invent
a new destination. Of course,
Renee will get there first.

Here and now I enter the room with watering eyes.
The name Dar is enough to move me: evidence of the living

invading the present to declare what matters
is what matters here and now. I am the tearful

subject mystifying the content. We are all the feeling
subjects asking for whom we promise the future.

> *I am a body*
> *in which feeling*
> *is foreign (sound).*

I am speaking to what hails me
to accompany fiction's sightseer.
We are in the middle
of an alarming departure.
I am becoming envious of the book
's stony bulk, of everyone I know
and their responses to the book
's gothic hieroglyphs, of everyone I don't know
and their saucy skywriting
above the straining church spires.
I am becoming a red-faced citizen
transported by desire.

A woman talking to a book is here and now.
A woman is Athena and Psyche at the podium

proposing
an orgy.

We cannot be surprised if two or more of our muses
take up the call. It's theory in practice.

Renee is the book I am reading:
but Coolidge's *The Crystal Text*
surprised me out of a daydream one winter afternoon;
Olson's *The Maximus Poems*
arrived in the mail like a frantic black poodle
shivering too manically for me
to understand how I should address it.

Renee is the book I am speaking to.
We are on the other side of meaning now.
Elegy asks a lot of time

and life. Rice left sitting on the counter overnight
bears an enormous grudge. Like all women,
the architects wanted a private room for the chiding.
The book is being carried off by militant house ants.

Renee is the book I am writing:
a squirming genealogy
of the memoirists, dramatists, and cinephiles
from whom I steal singing men like Simon.

Herculean muses lift their hem lines
to reveal the ruffles underneath. The air is abuzz

with the sound and the stench of mourning.
The wind is a brisk reminder that our grandmothers

possessed a second sight. Poverty transforms
the dandelion into something terrible.

I am under that bookcase
still with Lorine and Virginia. Reaching for Renee.
I am standing on my stoop in Montréal
la retentissante and receiving lashes
from the mailman. He has the slender build
and neat black moustache I imagine Simon
to possess. I am about to climb the mountain.

I plunge my head
into the forgotten pit
into which future and allegory
drive the earth into watery space.
Do you understand
the mechanics by which
the ground becomes sky?

Our new constellations "Long skirt, belonging to Virginia" and "Sensible pants, worn to seams by Lorine." For a brief moment, the book halts. I am talking to it as a method of arriving in and, subsequently, transforming the present.

See how rapidly the body of the writer vanishes.

The room is sliced by sunlight built as it is
with spacious gaps. A child's treehouse

of leftover 2x4s. The father harumphed
and the preferred daughter placed her new wife behind

the miniature kitchen set. Dandelion soup is no
joke. Still, there is the hope of laughter uncoerced.

In the badly formed guise of an author
tapping a perverted historical document onto a screen
I climb the crude staircase
and enter childhood's kingdom. I find the appropriate tone
— *yellow and windy* —
to mock the good name of literature.
The present cannot make its entrance
here and now.
I am climbing nothing
other than the debris of a gutted
mini home. Ham radios a plastic bag containing
other plastic bags and a single ceramic plate.

This is my fictional autobiography of reading.

I have failed to sublimate anything.

Risk Writing It Down

I feel the needle prick on my white recollection.
My fecund jowls emit a childish whisper
where the jovial silhouette absconds.
Halfway to the island, my ode becomes
a startled cry. Mud, shore,

some sailboat drifts. Mother's cotton dress
billows into the essential body
or memory. Yes, it takes
the shape of the hammer. I am one
of many mutants in the commemoration.

What I am not reciting is innumerable
            blood, body and
            delight, definition of
            love, infant conclusion about
            party, the nurses'
            sex, a woman's
            understanding, mirror of

            arse, a feather in the
            hazard, game of
            men, inferiority to
            prescription, signed
            remains, chapel containing
            smallness, sign of
            skirts, Mother's

I once knew a ghost (the bishop)
who flew over sweetly green hills
while sweating full-proof whiskey.
Who in this family can help the blind drinking?

I think of the turbulent welter
in his moth-eaten pockets. Jam-soaked remnants
on the spirit body. My mother once took pity
and sewed his papers to the cloud-wisp collar.

They spelled out the congregation's jealousy
air, given a disturbed
darkness, cast in
foreign, free sale of
hand, in her other
viscera, viscous and black
wanted, whose return

amends, making
applause, receiving limited
burst, about to
eagle, ready for the spread
encountered, like nothing you've
intention, without
non-existence, plane of
tease, not a

The next of kin is not a friend
but what disturbs them
is welcome. I preferred being unspayed.
A godmother, like you, with no choice but to dance.

The Factory Missile

I like being used by the machine.
I like being its little wife.

My body was never flesh entirely.
And yes, it is Simon, he writes me
with news of the belching cicadas.

Who else?
Lorine and Virginia crowd into our flying minivan.
We are on a road trip to the largest commemorations
of produce: blueberry, potato, artichoke.
When we arrive at the eighteen-foot wheat stalk,
Renee is already there, gnawing its waxy waves.

Begin it.
Virginia and Lorine are cloaked in scurrying whispers
and staring at my shiny pink hunchback.

I understand him (Simon).
It's no small thing
to write in the other.

We are delivered to the wealthy town lush
with opportunity. I am awash
with aptitude. Listen as the record unfolds
and tell me I am wrong
to cast myself in the divine role.

Listen, Simon, do you not want that I live my life?
Lorine and Virginia are tiring of our shenanigans.
See how they ignore us to sing their arias.

To meadowsweets I rise open. Turn twice where
we briefly copulated. In the open-air galleria.
Virginia and Lorine, I make my apology to you here
in the middle of the artificial green.
Look how the staff placed plastic dandelions
under our feet. We will be walking on neon
yellow petals for all our lifetimes.

We want it all debris. I want it all, the world,
complicit with the mouth. I want this
moneyed municipality to drain its abundance into the hollow
between our large white teeth and protruding tongues.

My intention is to satisfy myself ten times within the hour
all day long for the entire month of March and every month
after that until my body becomes visible to all.

East of the street where nothing happens everyone
is their own happening. Everyone
is dressed in words
like "untrammelled," "blabber," and "ill-accustomed."
Simon, take me to bed
and leave my mind alone.

—

In the dream-palace constructed by Renee I am bullish.
I understand to have friends is faster.
I could possess a body like a socialite's
and gain a multitude. I have the necessary talents.
You know this.

I always thought the same thing. Simon and I.
We would change the world
with our untrammelled love-making. We forget. We need.
Lorine is teaching Virginia
to boogie-woogie.

The name I was writing was nothing not anything.
It needed roses. The name
I was writing had yet to arrive
but it was there. I follow it. I need a new mistake.

I loved Simon.
I thought I loved Simon. I knew a kind of love
when I looked into the sweet round face of Simon.

Taste it.
I became small.
It's a way of loving.

It's the buzz of a woman
saying, "If I do not love you absolutely
I will walk out without myself."

An entirely wanted one.
This is what I will walk out and become.

Inherited Smallness

I am seeking the means for transubstantiation
all simmering. My special sweetness

is an upside-down bat. Have I toppled over a balcony?
This one, no. But if we feel behind the present surface

we'll find a miniature self with her face to the sky
and his spine a strike against archaeology.

The silk kerchief is listening to the nervy recitation of facts:
"I fell," I'll say if saying it will win me love.

I am in the habit of building reality. As no one,
I was fertilizing the satisfaction draped over

our monogamous thrall. Luxury! I wanted to nose
this into the air like honey before the harm of men

returned, but the trouble with sermoning began again.
My aluminum siding was plenty reflective of meaning,

yes, but this was at the cost of freedom and softness.
How do I stand the dullness? While kneading the dough

for my breakfast, a feast of daylilies and resignment,
I remember: Buttons! These are always on her mind

so I add them to his running list, singing softly as I elbow
the whiteness. My folks are visiting soon.

Life will be low then.

Desire's Child

I am telling Virginia and Lorine about the analyst's prognosis.
They are pulling agonized faces. Lorine unties
the rose sash at her waist and stuffs either end in her ears.
Virginia upturns our pitcher of basil lemonade.
Citric rivers pass overhead.

I persist, telling no one in particular (Renee),
my migraines
are the manifestation of an unrooted boy,
ruddy-cheeked and wind-thin. I imagine
entering his sanctuary.

> *it was the home of a bad man*
> *his blood is mine*
> *tho the house*
> *is home*
> *it is forever*
> *in the mind*
> *torched and vacant*
>
> *the grey buildings had sound*
> *ghost chickens*
> *pig remnants*
> *& a place*
> *for hiding*
> *destroyed dolls shredded books*
> *the rocking chair's incestuous romance*

Virginia throws her heavy skirt
overhead. Lorine snores loudly
while apparently wide awake.
I give up the caress.

But I maintain the weaving,
scenes from the past driven mad by fiction's nosing,
telling no one in particular (my mother)
I have trespassed into myth's sky.

he is frightened
of me
I am child & man
w/ animal mind
fixed on desire
oil-soaked rags for the mouth
tongue tip to eyeball

he lets me feel
his scorching
& lets me soothe
his heaving
o how does the song go
fish chips vinegar
pepper pepper
salt

The women are an impasse against which I sing.
I am the unrooted boy,
sky-high in the golden coop. I am
becoming his sweet twin.

We Need Women

But they are not necessary to make me come.
If I were committed the thing would be done.

There was the desire to bike.
I began talking outside the book binding.

My pea know if I had not been with you —
the accident still would have happened.

In what way is tomorrow what I already know?
My pea I'm a bit tired but you're mad.

If I were already inside it I would not know the taste.
Vanilla spray and cold metal softening into hilarity.

How do people go on living?
Call it spectacular love.

The open mouth and its gravel.
I come to you as a ruin.
Indexed and blinking.

This is about yesterday's consequence.
Split self or sad sack. Why do I cry
when she presses my hips?

Monday I'm almost national.
I'm reconstructing some freedom.
Each inefficiency is radical by tomorrow.

There is a countenance gathering.
This is the land of every moment.

Neither life nor its green parks have been built.
Still I am happy with what sun and chess remain.
My pea there is no particular you I write to.

Wednesday I'm the daycare's feast. Little hands inside
the best parts of me. I'm remembering.
I possess a core. I'm keeping it.

I took want in my mouth and knew what it was to be rising.
Sunday bread crumbling in the red palms. Razing the city.
My sea urchin I woo the muscle of infertility.

The Wit of This Is Their Own

The queen mother thrusts
    my hand in the waters
    of her afterbirth:
Ambition
    here is your wide reverence
    a curse worn and old

Bolt upright I
    kiss the brocades
    the glistening stiletto —

the cannon shot of heirs
    a tender triumph
    in women's hearts

Memory tells me
the wars
will return to the cabinet
but for now my water-logged hand
is engaged to elegies

Yellow
is my victory

In birth and all that follows
there are those served
and those serving

My lie is to be neither
    I am a sickly hand
    in the muck of nobility

The croaking memory of History
in musty furs
pledging loyalty
To my viciously whispering muses

Nothing Compares to Your Waistline

The colour is midnight. Worn across the barrel chest of my men.
Against this is the white gold of women's nudity. A great crowd
of motherless daughters. All the more profane for the sheer
fabrics touching nipples. These pink prods swing and stamp.

One more jump and the floor will cave. So, jump! Take us,
the motherless river cries. Into the basement where the men
's skirts turn up. Two long legs in blue plaid kick a cigarette
into the fainted lad's mouth. A haze of smoke. A sudden high
-resolution nightmare.

Men in bristling suspenders. Women in kitten heels. Lorine
and Virginia dancing in ill-conceived steps. The floorboards
are sound. The stage is theirs. Their fourteen eyes winking
at me in technicolour. The audience bobs its purple wigs.

Dream changes scenes. Virginia is in a director's chair
making a note on the clipboard in her lap. Lorine is swinging
from the hot, blinding lights. In the blaze, men are stomping
the heaving film reels. I am overjoyed.

The soundstage is a wild garden. Lorine and Virginia
exchange their scripts with a troupe of men
for their night-capes. Modernist women and denuded men
descend the balcony staircase in Lindy Hops. I am the ornate
golden clock offering the sun-tanned procession
a measure for living.

Nudity becomes window dressing. The women are waiting
to be eaten up. The non-existent waifs tied into suffocating
brassieres and hip-gliding skirts. All sewn up
with an entire continent's silk.

I am the gloved white hands of the titleless mass tracing
latitude and longitude. Searching for the dewy banks.

I am the knee at odds with the marble floor
of the basement's catwalk. The splitting sound prompts
the teeming masses to press their chests into the window glass.

All shatters. All dancers are now crowned, glimmering
dust in their hair like so many tiaras. Virginia shakes her mane
with equine grace. Lorine pulls the locks
into her mouth. I'm inspired to colour my shag.

In the black-and-white reprieve, Lorine greases
her shoe bottoms. Virginia rearranges her ermine muff.
Shining like scorched grass.

My men are undressing and drawing on their well-
oiled bodies the tuxedos of the first night's dancing.

Take us, my men, yodel. Clutching the ends of their pigtails.
Take us as we are. Little boys performing our tricks in ruffles.

Take us, Virginia and Lorine whisper. Their tone is viscous.
Take us as we are. Retreating at speeds I cannot capture.

I am dipping the mic to the floor. Their skittering footsteps.
Their dripping sweat. It is pleasure. It is discipline.

Dar's Rosy Cheeks

Dear ritual,
the dreams in which I spoke a language I could
                                        not understand
are in the doorway awaiting greeting.
Can you, before dawn bends into her plié,
find for them something to do? Their nametags
say "cry lemons, suck tears,
bark into the future, take direction..."

Maybe it is not true that the language gives me
                                        difficulty
my landmark is the little, red-clay dog statue.

Smiling like a cadaverous horror machine,
but loving Nature and visiting hotels and carrying
                           binders of government papers
flightless strawberry-jam-pecked rags cocktail
into the morning's good will
      "Hi. Bonjour."
Blows to the head
I like to begin my day with black water and lead
as if working the elements into my magic
I mean, my body

Ritual, did you receive the day's warning?
"Blue eyes carry clarity,
or clarity plucks the tongue of the child,
the old lane is pure muck, impassable,
we lie down in the sentiment..."

The direction of our desire is barking mad
custom foolish unrecognizable inheritance
take my dream in marriage

speak to me in a language I understand
with a body like the sun's rolling tears.

Architecture is Indistinguishable from Cunning

I'm the father of entering the world.

To the little girl
of the underworld
lambs have talons.

Renee, I'm plummeting.
I can only sop up
so much.

As a father, I am amazed; what I shoot changes. The way I
video conference innocent as an enforcer.
The lambs want to police this.

My litter is voluminous; I let them write
our ramshackle autobiographies. Their blabber
is the language of the feral. I own it.

I make a little movement left.
To transform shadow into screen.
I will re-emerge complete.

The way of the witch but straight.

Renee, I now think
all this talking is not
reaching your avian ears.

I sacrifice the furred litter.
This is a joy, for I know
they will never be orphaned.

In above messages the concern is other.

I choose to teleconference with my head in the bath.
The result is unsurprisingly damp. My ears newly electric.

I found a way to collect unemployment insurance
from three separate addresses while completing overtime
from a fourth.

The sky changes colour
after the flood.

Renee, I confess
to having failed then quit
fourth level swimming.

I took the long way back to see the party.

I composed a lengthy text to my mothers before dropping
my phone off the fortress tower.

Go, the people say
it is time.

After the flood come the others.

Yes always a moral document of my entering the world.

I'm My Own Little One

I would agree with the oceans in the dispute.
To possess a wave is to be divine.
I read of ritual use.
The guidebooks promised that the old master sat
bare-assed every day in his favourite vinyl booth.
I suck the lies out.
The guidebooks promised a canal in the desert.
The water thick with pink joy.

Tonight
I order risotto
and go for
the prosecco.
Tonight
I wear the shirt
of the man
who stuck his flag
in my back.
How sharp
the prongs of nationalism,
so like the long prologue
of romantic love.

The news
every six hours.
It's 7:00
and I have
everything. It's 3:14
and the black hag has
my big toe in her mouth.

This exists. Sidewalks and
dustbins and the word “noise”
on telephone
poles. Peroni
and sliced ham and soldiers’
uniforms. A real mind.
Enflamed by the anomalous population.
Inventing it and invented by it.

In order to be cultural
I buy a new hat.
My mother taught me to love
an accumulation.

Disappointment
emerges in everything.
My mother
again. She emerges
in everything.
                    Anything can end up ruining a real mind.
Scandal here is prompt.
Sorrow is tartar
on my keyboard.

Listen
to the TV.
What you are hearing
is a shift in mood.
You tasted it first.
Listen to the forest
of envy. What you are hearing
is a black hair in the hand.
You steamed it. Three blocks
from the building and I
call the doctor. Yes

I'm now on his time.
No I'm not too busy.
I'm my own little one.

Now I leave
the doctor's palace defiant
and drumless.

                    What sounds do our bodies make? Silken
yellow chicks melting into the cake's glaze. Ear tips
burning on top of the artisanal canoe. Whose bodies
do these sounds eviscerate?
Among men I am never

not small.
Among women I am never

myself. Among children
I am the bowl of gruel.

                    I am interrogating my relationship to form
and deciding in favour of formlessness.

          I am failing
to convey it plainly. You and I
are in love, but this
does not eradicate the claim
of the man and his close twin.
It's 6:45 or 17h10.

   First of all it depends on whether I
intended to send
my grandmother
to slaughter.

Oh what disturbs me is
also welcome.
It is you. You are
always welcome.

In my last book my mother
was disappointed to find
so much sex in what I
intended as violence.

            First I was a deity; then, a feral orphan boy;
then, the saviour invented as a lie by the man;
now, finally, I am the matchstick girl of your dreams.

                    Our bodies, banners in the new order,
leave ample room for questions. Our bodies:
yours and mine.
Yes this is my entire world.

Will You Remake My Mortality?

The trimmings were becoming more and more wrong
for the day trilled of grief rather than splendour.

Renee, I'm plummeting. You catch me in arms
as willowy as Virginia's.

I looked up into the candied planets and forgave them
their seasonal cacophony. I could now imagine
my destiny in a shape other than flagellate failure.

Virginia, I speak to you as snow
is creeping into privileged doorways.

You pull on a fur hat and become
the exact image of Lorine.

I am shouting into the domed ceiling
of my own fat head. I made, in my sudden
ecstasy, as if I would leave the frozen ground.

Lorine is a name for green dreams. I speak to you
and time passes.

Heels dangling in the fetid summer air, I strained
upward; my seat remained as if fastened
to its supple leather cushion. Useless,

unchanging, mortal, I hurled these words
into the dome; *old pig, crone, dullard*;
and the green balls exercised their ethereal care.

Three retreating books thrum as a multitude.
All new women in less than contemporary costume.

Saturn drank their words as if prayers.

I made, in my new drunkenness, as if I would leave
my library. Mind a burgeoning sphere behind
the refrigerator I clasped my hands and applauded.

Like a holographic glitch we are three
the women and their lovers and I.
I could resituate the quivering ethics
between the weighty desire and its expressive refusal.
As the swarm, you took the red dirt into heaven song.

The Dawn about to Be Ushered in

left-handed friend   in lightning you are solace

                    metal hurling (digging frog ponds)

air rides the current between

                    yr flashing eyes & my swollen thumb

air

                    hurls crystals into sticking time

                    red & throbbing time says

                    a lapse in sense-making will do good

red-throbbings laugh at my planless lives

red & throbbing time chose to invade

                    the night, revolting

                    I am dulse-covered & over morning

our unsynchronized friendship enters new territory

yr eyeballs wide & yellow

my thumb forever demanding

my nation, be free

by the light of your absence I am learning a kind of sobriety

without result

without focus   without deprivation

without way-time

14 centuries & the hurling-wind is still dividing us

crystalline sheets of air

hand everything to nightfall

my body diminishes

my body is red & throbbing

Virginia, take my thighs to the moon

Lorine, take my left breast   take it to the swamp

you, friends, must make me   small

unnamed

& wonderful

Enjoy the Work

Do not open the work. This is the advice left for you:
DO NOT OPEN THE WORK.

It's true that long after all that pain I need a reward.
Yes. Yes. I need a reward.
To accept nothing
is to wear an historical face. History is dead.
The scowling tenant dies in flagrant defiance of history.
In the growing flames the library continues to collect debt.

I wrote it out as if I would live forever
if I only wrote more often.
This was a false impression.
Otherwise the lost one would have written the book.
How far I've gone in this conversion.

I was holding back from saying it. The wild lair
was keeping all warm and moist.
If I could form the words
they would have talons. This implies
wings and violence. I was holding

myself at fourteen years old. Air stream girl
hiding her mouth and clutching her locked diary.
My mother's mother found a way to open me.

Money for sex, sweat for beauty, flesh
for the cat's love. What's mundane is intimate
with History too.
I am from a long line of dandelion-eaters
who know how to spin thin air into the stuff
of reality. The cavern soul makes the transmutation sweet.

Have you joined me on the bridge?
NOBODY MOVES UNDERNEATH.

I know I am fortunate to be calculating the future.
I wanted to have friends
but I'll accept the erection
of a statue in my honour. Better that strangers
unaccustomed with my rude breath construct my likeness.
I know I've gotten away from reality again.
I mean, I know you think of our bodies as closed systems.
I tell you how wrong you are by blowing one modest kiss.

My mother's mother knew a smile larger than the mouth.
Keep it going. This thing called living
or driving or supplementing the income of the rich.
Make learning to swim a priority.

To go on living might require more than sex,
beauty, and the cat. Underneath this, where stillness
is snarling propinquity, you expected more. Lately
I am embarrassed by the obvious effort
of pleasured people. I love your bristling demeanour
but I would like you to recognize how
unreasonable you've been. I did not say the bridge
would hold us. Let wetness in.

You are learning well. You are learning.
NOTHING MOVES UNDERNEATH.

Our mothers warned us that writing it down carried risk.
We changed the direction and the risk grew wilder.

Those Unheld

I once laid more flexible tiles in this life
You were a flexible treasure

I treasure an Earth with carrots and small copies
You could sink the POV using night as yarn

I think furniture and governability are no more valuable
Than a carrot. With you I rid the small sinks of their clogs

My talking must reach the ears of a multitude
I keep it. I keep it

I tried to build it after you. Your absence made it

I failed to make it on my own
I set it adrift and prayed it would sink to the depths

Your city is dressed in aquamarine words. Its citizens
Have gills. My conscience is clear

My conscience is a suffragette sash
I wear it over my drooping right breast

Behind the teeth a new world. A cave begging entrance

I speak as if the heart has some influence. Holding loss
Under my tongue. Poison candy for the bawling babes

Why should I be innocent in the longing hours when you
Cannot know. If your auntie messaged the rats of Hampstead

My ecology is on the way to they-ness
To learn the name is fantastic

People like the valves of the cosmopolitan
People like you and me

How can we be certain that our making two or more is pleasing
While you're right it does not matter I want the line symmetrical

Have I apologized. My sorrow is well-fed

My line of becoming curves just there where you place a finger
I am as becoming as any lady-in-waiting

But less so than the cigarette hanging limply from smirking lips
Less so than a pair of velvet green armchairs

The way to borrow the name of pharaohs is to make a vow
To learn the name is original is to be told to wait

I spit in the leafless face of the people
Your city really does have faith

You could have faith in people
In the valves of the cosmopolitan

People like you and me

Horizontal thought can come to you without complaint
I dance along behind its wide gait

I am standing at your city's entrance or I think I am
Without squares or citizens it is hard to be a city

Careful. Careful

If the two of us really made it work at the salt mine
We planned to touch the surprise of the computer

People do not know anything without morning
All longing is actual

People like you and me

Families are onerous things totally without grace
Mouth twisted in perpetual want

If love could enter the world without a match
You too may learn to swoon

My mentioning the jacket brought to life an elasticity
If you could attend the thought

Is it privé. The flattening feeling
When we address the fact you are alive no longer

Holding you would ossify it

You are now a woman with my mother's name
Father's sister or grandmother's mother

Acquaintance's missed connection. No matter the ruby cheeks
You are Queen Charlotte scolding me

Adoring me. Could it be so
I think I can read your mind. All is censored

Mother, come back to me. I want a new name

Softly paddling into the lover's nightmare
I share my fantasy of absolution

The black-hatted actuary. My star-studded avatar
You should have stuck around for the discovery of the cure

Without vertical understanding the nameless citizens
Are blameless. So abundance is the problem

Amputated. I can't avoid the fact. Wounding you
Made me a person unlike the one I knew

In the faces of the Charlottes. This was alarming
And irresistible. I am still open to reconciliation

Are you

WHEN A FOLK, WHEN A SPRAWL

Where Are We

Memory is a gift-in-exchange

I give the fraud your found-sound

The mom-moan. Whose guff called the doctor

Freud snoozes in the window

I sought the perfect gift

To give the doctor. I found the flowers

To mow down the memory

The lost mother and the two wives

The father. The fraud

It was a potato. Ready-rot it was

Green or mostly

My father was a man. Carved the thing

Insisted the ruin was good. To eat

Eat it raw. My father was a man

Delivering a lesson. As a man

The moral was waste not. To want more

I took it well. I swallowed it

There is love in the room. I lean

Into the cough. The lilacs drop

These flowers don't rhyme

The tip of my nose cold. Into the deep-freeze

The white behemoth. As tall as me

A child. The oldest of three

My mouth wants cardboard. My ears want blue

SUPER VANILLA PEANUT-FREE

Alone in the party-scene. Spilling with invisible light

Two hands and the sibling mirrors

Did my moan have purple. In its winnowing

The ready-rot of consciousness. Keeps my nose cold

Three of us rode

Whose rough-guise. Whose road-gyre

The smoke made it so

The wuzz-or-whir. The monologue will not revive

My memory of her

Three of us drove. The night's machinations

For twenty-eight long days. It was only May

The stench visible. In the glass

Would the lilacs be in bloom

I take it into the mouth. The fur-ball

Heel-toe the descent

There are no directions. To follow

Slip into the mind

Whose voice in my ear. My mother

Came into the room

When I least expected it. Mid-morning

Light

In the mouth the myrrh. Becomes gold

Whose glance

My moan. Travels at moon-speed

My mother has planned

A feast. Crocus and hyacinth

Five Generations of Wheel Women

I.

Will you take me there, little one?
The dirt beneath your lady's feet is white
Where I was born it is red
Women are more likely to wear a crow as a hat
Than slide their slick tits into wire
Where I was born women move like water over grass
Inside you are perfectly
Ordinarily you
A squat mystery of profound proportion
Silver beads penetrate the space between
You and me
Over you ladies move deep
Into the forest thick with flies
Wearing wide-brimmed hats

My neck is damp
I place the cool of my hand there
You
You are unmoved
No string connects you
You and me
Your images of past wealth
My tits loose
My hair a diminished poof
The day's heat burning up your silver hooves
My painted feet in great-grandmother's vegetable garden
I learned to deadhead carrots with my teeth
I learned to laugh until all the family we pissed our pants
We saw the streams running down our legs

II.

Little one
Was it you
Just now
That cough
Would you care
To interject
What have you
To say
What were you
Before you
Were you
Here
And
Now

I am chewing
The scent
Pig-shit
Remembering
Old Nana
The grinning statue
Can't see it
Through the stench
I am lapping up
The spanks
Little shits
That's me
And
The locked child

III.

You show me

The dirt drove. The woman-child mad
The damp poof. Radish halves

Greens soaked in vinegar. Profound sound
Strong between. The house and the trailer

They burn those who cough. String them up
In the hot sun. You were born

To sizzle without proof

I was born. To snow drifts
Catapult of engine drowning. Father flung

Calf head kept whole. A fortune spent
On refrigeration. Ample bottoms

You and I. Snapping dirt-streaked asparagus
In order to breathe. With madness running free

IV.

You and I both

Born from dirt. Returning to it. Grass up the bottoms
Our pretty pink feet. Burn up the notions

That pelican is profound. The lawn's proportions
All wrong. Hoist those girls up with a bra

Girl! Shut the doors to the damp. Eat the carrot
Straight from the dirt. Heads in the sand

Bums against the tree trunk. Profound!

Ankles crossed behind the knees. Greening the body
Licking the finger's mayonnaise. Cut it out. Man

I told you. Sitting soggy in the basket like that
Our father's swimming shorts. Putrid shell

Fire against the low tide. Bikini tops untied
Sand knows our insides. Keening. Let the moonlight come

V.

Oh, they can't see an eye for it
They are up to their elbows
In the dirt of you and me
Don't let no damp inside those doors
Don't let no damp
Inside
Oh, little one, this voice
Is it any remedy?
No! Cough into the elbow
Poof! You are outside. Poof! You are a squat
Little one with no string. This too shall pass
Why did I expect you to soothe me?
Pristine and ungiving you became
Why did I expect anything

My tits are toddling
From the pantry into the kitchen
They are siblings
With uneven haircuts
You are the family portrait
Me and my tits arranged
Under hot Sears lights
My great-grandmother is dusting the frame
Singing lowly to the child
Locked up in the back room
It's only my imagination
Constraining the infantile woman to damp silence
My imagination faces its early death
In a separate room into which we moved the family portraits

An Instinct Says Tune It Out

I am bottoming all blue in the face
It's all decay the taste in my mouth
What slithers out is this: "That bastard —"
It's true all but the foundation burned
They built up the unsound bottom
"Bottoms up!" My uncle was 7-years-old
When he jumped off the roof
Fell to the ground and did not soar
Broke two knees — "That bastard"
The older brothers swore
They were not responsible
Both father and mother
Long since decomposed
Watch over the boys
The ancestral home watch it burn
Watch it burn — "Poor Mum
She didn't deserve HIM!"
It's true all children will believe in flight
To fly requires one long jump
My uncle was 7-years-old
When he jumped off the roof
The wasted life I stop to taste it
I stop it moaning I lie in the yellow grass
My 7-year-old uncle turns darkly
Sees me sees a stranger and opens his mouth
To stop it the warp
My 7-year-old uncle stands outside the blue light
He is a man traffic roars past a glint of unknowing
He spits out the names of the older brothers
He does not know me he does not know me
Promises of love were lacunae for mum
"She didn't deserve him!"

Alcohol oceans of it took them
Washed the names of the older brothers from his mouth
My uncle turned darkly to face the lacunae
“Didn’t deserve it”

A red sunset is delight and moonshine
The men are soon coming home
My secret is the shoebox of paperbacks
My sister’s is that she read them too
Is there anything like a tree house in the sky?
Should I encourage the little sister to eat
The grass kept in the sink fourteen long winters?
She is trying to keep her skull intact
I hear her whispered sutures
Sitting with my friends the trees
Soon our home will be revealed: I am sure of this
Without knowing the word “climate”
Without knowing the word “narcissism”
Naked rooms for the distant roaring
Our bunkbed thumpings on display
The little sister had nowhere to hide
Our mother’s instinct is to go on writing
At the kitchen table — a vertical notepad
Placed squarely over the astrology section
Rising dust clouds from the dirt lane
Are too great a lure
Our mother is keeping
Our little brother a secret
She stands at the door of our newly visible home
Her two girls are in the dirt
With newly arrived criminals
Our mother opens the collar of her blouse
Readjusts her torment
She redirects the newcomers

Away from the grins of her daughters
Our mother is making a promise
In a language I am unable to fathom
I am sticking my fingers in the ears of my little sister
She is repaying the favour
How to account for sound disappearing?
Our mother returned to the kitchen table
Rust in the atmosphere like a veil pulled

I was speaking
To no one other than myself, my sister, and our mother
My whole world and its burgeoning expansions
I went on as though praying in the bishop's home
Bernard was the name I whispered fervently
"How can I know..." I asked the beads
Pooling in my palms — "You make me feel...
The fortune is gone... The graveyard has it."
This was the embarrassment of too-little
Among trees I knew protection
In the roaring highway traffic I knew my uncle
He was gone
I was standing at midnight in a blue robe
The little sister was drumming the top bunk with her heels
Bernard is the name
"The kitchen is gone... We've made it subterranean."

Swam a River, Struck a Stone

Okay my truth derives from the peony
the peony is an event like a miracle
the pleasure and the pain are not fictions
language is the truth of the peony
The peony's feeling proud, this day is its last

yeah that's the boreal feeling hanging like yellow
vapours in the air as if all is ordinary

The word "palpable" makes departure possible
makes me minimally blue in the face
makes me luxuriate in the torture and remission
I place the blame
on the bathers in the drooping pith
thrumming with the hiss of pursuit
I am reassured by stuffing the journal into the suitcase

Kill the hush keep the bull survive the inspection
penned in with a push I soar
oh the gate oh the pursuit oh the many people
flowering hot like steel before I am delivered

Okay the truth of it —
what do I know of the peony I know it is yellow
what I expect is a blue and pink crowd
submerged in water its cut stem its glass

Straining upward a cloud detached
the pleasure of tenderness in the fold oh
the pain pulls down on it
the pride knows no give

Making it blue in the face pink and sick of it
what do I know of the pain I know what I feel

If It Rots

Won't it rot like that   like what
Well won't it   I put the compost out

On Tuesday nights I put the compost out

The city asks it   the city asks if

I have managed the problem of the black mold

I had not been told   I had not been
Told of any such problem   Mold?
In the kitchen sop it up   the pooling pink shadow
Fresh halibut   in the kitchen sop it up
That's flavour, there!   My father says it
Flavour! inside my mind   Flavour! outside the city
The red island says it   Fresh halibut! Say it
The paper says it's $7.49/lb
Was this fair?   A fair price? Was it?

Now in the kitchen I work my mouth around
F L A Y   —   V E E R

This was long past the waking rays of morning light
When the bare kitchen offered me toast (black)
Coffee (white)   a cooling tile
The underside of my bare feet   toes painted pink

The night was no rose but it bloomed

In the kitchen sop it up
The fish no good
Doused it, she did!
Doused it in what?
Salt (sop it up)
In the kitchen
The night offers no gold
No taste (sop it up)

the pooling pink shadow
my cooking no good
My father says this
Oil (pooling)
Pepper (too little)
the century's shadow
no luxury (too little)
no love to be sold

The night is a glass in which I can squint and

see her face
Long green nose
Is it a glass?
I throw it to the floor —
It shatters

Aflame

When did she get so old?
pinched purple lips
or the cover of a book?
it's a vase
the once cool tile
(old refuge)
the refractory pink bloom

Oh, Anne — won't you say it again?
You knot yourself up
this way and that in the wind
or the windless day of summer
hot — without relief

Won’t it rot like that — won’t it?
But the problem is — the thing’s done
The thing’s empty — it’s nothing
Not even decay will grow — So what’s this about mold?
It’s the cooling tile — kitchen morning, afternoon
Anne prefers it — flavourless

The day turns — I confront the living
my body waves back
I catch it — in the mouth

Of the night
It is now
The night, of —

Oh, Anne — what was it you said again?
The words vanished as soon as they appeared
cool pristine bubbles on the soda’s surface
no — dandelion wisps in a child’s breath
nose smudged with red dirt, always
always the nose smudged and the eyes screwed up

In the blackness I strain my eyes and

stop my ears — plug my nose
pinch my lips — catch it

The night is no rose but it blooms

Everything Appeared in Its Tenderest Form

It was in search of a horizon that I lost my home. I knew something as a child, before my eyes went wandering and my ears were the next to leave, when I could not taste how a star sets the mind straight. Life keeps on as if I want it tragic. I keep the radio on. My home becomes known.

I seek no heat
no comfort

I try hard to be smooth
beam or be

I see

Would such a bird
seek

the concrete solace
Sell out

or in

what would I be
truthful

what truth
have I

I see worms
all over

Hello, you,
how thick is it

Mown down
or blasted

All of it

have you said it
well, lie

it won't kill you
not likely to

Home was a place of frog sounds smaller than a child.
Darkness suited the shame. My body assented to what
came next. I think that if I can get the tingling back
I'll know my home. A place to be alone and jabbering.
A country-music beacon. Music and the television on.

I ask: so what
blot it out

blot it out
so what

say it
you ask: what

last century's straw hat
its splinters

its white leavings
the unfettered stars

bathroom carpet
no vacuum

any old truth
say it

something to darken
say something

forbidden place
was it

humidity
in that place

it lived
it lived, strangled

uncovered head
skeletal hands bashful

stick into
the corkboard

three sticking wheels
humid breeding

whose screen glows

have at it then
your dark sigh

it's only a part
of it (truth)

A child's imagining contained my body. I was a woman knowing the cruelty of the world. My ears the child. To know what it's like to carry a mouth, I go to the fathers. Like gods, their interference will be minimal. My known home. A technicolour banner.

I feel it — Can you —
you can

It is my cadaverous home
you see

My will to be
whole

Inside a being
my will to be

No-thing

Sepia!
Where have you gone

Walked away
Ran away

My mind
no-thing to see

Please —
you see my home

Worms in corners
you see I'm home

truthfully
I could be

a part
of it

the end (oh)
the end

the beginning
or the end

say it (something)
it won't kill you

not likely to
anyway

My Green Thoughts

Time is that in which an empty glass weighs heavily
Why is such a deconstruction not permitted
I like the idea of ceasing being

Why is the memory-home licked by flames
The stranger was crowned in silver foil
Her head in the tub with the threat of something feral

Cannibalize the companion and conjure away
How white its face
I aim for my heart

The stranger was a woman in rags and bruises
White porcelain and hydrogen peroxide
The sun would help her achieve her dreams

The thing is more blue than thought
Would it know if the sky fell
I have already seen the final stage of my decomposition

Two mothers in the small bathroom rinsing their mouths
I was one older daughter asking if the doors were locked
No safety in women changing their hair

Break open the old one
What is invisible inside the embrace
I pause to examine the nonsensical and the anachronic

No safety in children at the windows
I see him with infinity inscribed on his brow
Handing fire to unfinished home

The thing's cage sings of its desire of recognition
Should we note the weather
I note the weather. Its jubilance

Did we flee?

Create a trajectory for le temps
May the double peonies conquer the world
I follow the night's little predictions. Time stops

He was out there in the night: large, invisible, and menacing
Safety became a matter of locking eyes with the stranger
Keeping her scorched head in the tub

Harm made arrival an exact science

And we were in the way of badness and its sweet aroma

A non-believer at the magician's table

A glinting thing makes the pocket a world

Late at night gloom prevents the senses from multiplying

Give your eyes to pleading woman

Our silence is a prayer to be held close to the bosom

Two prowling cats are mewing into a heating vent

The bitch and its mother bark

Animals perk up like silver gongs

Night switches on with the readiness of the witch
Badness had the power to keep memory open
To be unromantic was to be swept away by desire

Engaged in pelting our stranger with fear's arrows
Her clavicle red through the eyes of lace
Two mothers putting their brood in danger's path

No safety unless undertaking a moral risk

The Poise That Knowledge Gives

In the story I was told
it is always too late for Eve.
The green field was no longer
playing host to fools.

Too late! The crown is high on discipline
and colour-elated. I cannot keep warm
in the favourable wind. So the consensus is:
Be careful! In the story I was told
Original woman does break through.
Eve funds the public's organizations
— well, I'll be — provides the ground
for grand revolt. Jesus, Joseph, and Mary.

Now the ground is soaked
in blood.
She's a hot piece
Eve
a jewel of a wife.
Holy Hannah! she's a hot one.
In the story I was told
it is the seventh sense by which the fathers knew
the air turned. Limestone cliffs and dragging skirts
are all the field could imagine, as well as
a woman's bare knee as big as the pyramids.
The divine bulldozers
stop cold.
Eve with the burning dictionary in her hands.

Like all women she is held
and killed by History.
I was told she took her poise
to the sky.

I cannot refuse truce.
To undulate unnecessarily
Eve
was guilty of that.
So the consensus is
I must veer towards
the future —
but quietly!

The stars go on shining.
Roasting!
The public's forceful neglect
takes her poise and toasts it —
Black.
It isn't like life is natural, it is simply
butterflies and rock,
living hard and by air.
Eve dared to imagine durable works.
Walking beside the trees
in the favourable wind, she was evenly following
the road
and wheel
when a carriage arrived.
And opened.

As a child
Eve played xylophone.
As a child
even she knew no peace

was possible.
Money mows down
the first original woman.
Eve provides the ground
for refusal. Today's flag is holy!
and X-rated!
My imagination joyed going about.
I simply felt nothing at all

about Santa Claus with his reindeer
in the space between the bed ladder
and the mirror frame. I saw his unbearded face
in the cards I threw down.
I am a woman but I go into pubs, for time allows it.
A snake warms itself on a sun-baked brick
and I remember Eve
living by rock and air.
I am a woman making ready for a last voyage out, as if
I dipped my hands into the gutters, as if
things happen at the back door — a boy drowns!
a fisherman loses first one arm
and then his brother!
a little stranger is thrown into the street!
I recall how it can be all this and more in summertime.

The Horse
died in the green field
of Memory. Grab the poison dart
and lift it to the wind

Eve and I could not
provide the necessary warmth
to keep the animal alive, to peer
into its cavern ears. The problem
was lodged firmly behind the skin.
Our chocolate companion was dead
before he had a name
by which we could mourn him. Fathers

enter the field and empty it
of life. I alone sweat. Eve sinks. Where carved letters
warn "no trespassing" I am the promised son
with golden breasts. I sit by the road,
I squat in the ditch,
tilting my head and wedging the dart
into my seventh sense.
Air turns cool underneath the sun's smirk, so
the fathers return home with their long arms retired, so
the original woman is properly admonished
and waiting up for them in bed. I am the golden child,
splitting my seams to fashion a dragging skirt. Now,
I am the empty field
and the memory of the Horse
Wind a low hum in the tentacled leaves

I Am the Gold Machine

I am made big
made small
unwell and deep inside the worm's hole
changing size and unable to feel the body
whole

once barren
now lush
will my companion look up from his work
my future in his lap

will my companion look up from his work
outside the day is wet with lush
green witches

inside the body is a smaller self
an infinity of mirrored selves
now made big
now made small
as separate beings my companion and I
we are affixed to the dais
hands in blessing
we are recuperating
any moment now we will bounce up
outside the mouth

reproductive technology makes it possible
to birth the self
the mess is small

any moment now the recuperative space
of the mind will flicker
the mind
made small

I am a child in a torn dress
with my genitals moving loosely in the far stream
not bothering to cover myself
for what child means is loved one
what genitals stand for are affinities

if you take your size too literally
my companion
you will drown in loose lust

I am running through the illustrated fields
of childhood with my loose genitals
and breaking off the choke-cherry leaves
and coming to that shoreline where you
my companion
are nodding off

into the recuperative space of the mind
a flicker

The water is as cold as May
I mean, Mae
the grandmother whose scolding hands
clutch the locked, unlocked
diary in which I wrote
well let's not touch that
too closely
the water is cold and I am an old man
bare ass plunging

another shore line is inevitable
at the end of the journey
if you move, as directed, to the east
or the west
but never both at once
we two are three
or many more
flagrantly lifting our robes
we become another size

I Come Back to the Geography of It

I was so young and my first memory
is of the grass spread at our feet
three children in tatters
was it one pair of jeans
shredded and re-stitched for our paltry shorts
surely not but in the memory we three are one
jean-clad kid with chest bared
to the sun hot
we are red in the face
and everywhere else red too
we are rolling in it
the dirt
lane

A speckless vehicle
sprays gravel in its approach
turns suddenly and barrels toward us
stops in the knot of lane
and the vesica piscis
that contains
we three
"Do you know,"
a disembodied voice is asking
behind hot blue glass
"where to find the healing springs?"
Mom bustles out from the home
spits
bustles back in
we three
staring into the hot blue glass
"Do you know,"
an emerging jaundiced face is asking

"where to find the healing springs?"
we three
bare our chest to the hot sun

We three
beam red
knocking elbows and knees in the dirt
lane
"Do you know,"
an emerging orange torso is asking
hanging askance in white linen
from the speckless vehicle
"where to find the healing springs?"
Mom bustles out from the home
one fist raised and offering
a constellation of routes
a map
of unnamed roads
"Bishop MacEachern's Miracle Water"
is the horizontal script
preceding an arrow
an illustration of a glorified swamp

Mom
one palm containing
a Campbell's Mushroom Soup can
emptied out and scoured
awaiting
as the masking tape and permanent marker suggest
a "Toonie Donation"
we three
secure in knowing
the healing springs
are a font of dirty water
and, most excitingly, tadpoles

we suffocated dozens
in our mason jars
we three
pulsing under the red sun
and flickering

I was so young and my first memory
is of the secret of healing
this mystery, the bustling mother
and the patchwork stranger
and the three-headed child

manifest
now
as one desiccated lime
I was so young and my body
is the jean veil

I Met Death's Unlikely Twin

It was no dream
Veils part for the waking girl
It was I upright and knowing the total unknown
I had seventeen years of life
I was full of it and overpouring
out the hotel window I crashed
and He was
[waiting

But He will not bother us any longer
for here is Erín fiddling
the radio knobs and Laura frowning
the sound discordant. The sound filling
the empty cup of my tumbling out
the hotel window [I crashed
into the long-limbed embrace of E
laughing leather-clad and gnawing
at some animal flesh
L remained motionless
but in the solemnity of her gaze allowed that
a child should be permitted into their present scene
Rushing head-strong into the busyness Erín
Gesturing calmly to what would come Laura
I had glass
embedded
in my knees
Four hands were plenty
for the repair

The all-female baths were cloaked in steam
so thick I can taste it now crème anglaise
Erín delightfully wiping the upper lip
Laura tucking the towel

I had not yet said a word to armoured E
and crowned L and I would not

E was speaking English, French, Galician
L was keeping a light grip on the portable radio
Joe Hisaishi conducted our dreams
[Before
these two showed up in the spectral night
I was about to tumble directly
into the neck of a foul bottle. After
their invention. Well I was naked
and gleaming. Wounded and dressed
with feminine ideals
I was having uneasy thoughts about desire
I was the property of a bad man
These two rode in on E's white steed
and as I recall it was L who suggested
[I rewrite
the encounter. That this was possible

Maybe He is there somewhere still. But
in the all-female baths we were goddesses
or many-gendered pages. We were nude
and gleaming. Our wounds. Open

In the distance. History was churning its
[windmills
and I had reason to ask my saviours
about their relation. But E went on
inventing tongues. L flooding the sound
with water's heavy lack. From the baths
we moved to a rocky and barren plain
Here my two saviours flowered
transforming from worm to bird. I watched
[two angels

take flight into a sky suddenly brocaded
[with dawn
I was standing outside my hotel window
I had the strength of a sword
gripped by the hands of decorated amazons
[united

NOTES

The poems in "Ravishing the Sex into the Hold" were first written in a workshop hosted by Gail Scott at the Université de Montréal. The conceptual and experimental basis of the workshop inspired me to dive into Virginia Woolf's *Orlando*. The time-travelling text became a high modernist wave upon which the new poems could surf.

The poems in "Do I Enjoy the Work?" derived from a period in which I felt I could not write. As usual, I read instead. Two rhizomatic and architectural works of that reading period provided the strange cadence of the first notes toward these poems: Clark Coolidge's *The Crystal Text* and Renee Gladman's *Event Factory*.

The poems in "When a Folk, When a Sprawl" were first composed during two online workshops facilitated by Hoa Nguyen in which we read, respectively, Lorine Niedecker's *Collected Works* and Charles Olson's *The Maximus Poems*.

Montréal la retentissante was a phrase gifted to me by William Vallières. "An Instinct Says Tune It Out" takes its title from Gladman, "Everything Appeared In Its Tenderest Form" from Woolf, and "Swam the River, Struck a Stone" from Niedecker. The final three poems take their titles from first lines in Olson's book. "I Met Death — He Was a Sportsman" is altered to dismiss Olson's dream-meeting with Death in favour of a dream-meeting with two more poets (Erín Moure and Laura Broadbent).

ACKNOWLEDGEMENTS

It is such a pleasure to work with Invisible Publishing. Thank you to the entire team. Norm, for your camaraderie and enthusiasm, thank you. Megan, for the care taken with *A Number of Stunning Attacks* and the vision to come with *Cut Side Down*, thank you.

Thank you, immensely, Julie Joosten, editor extraordinaire, for equipping me with the suffragette sash. You introduced me to the book I was writing.

I would also like to thank the following journals and presses for publishing early versions of some of these poems: rob mclennan published the opening poem as "The Violence of the Hammer Is Thrilling" in *Touch the Donkey*; ryan fitzpatrick's Model Press published a chapbook containing poems from "Ravishing the Sex into the Hold;" "The Factory Missile" and "I'm My Own Little One" were published in *Always Crashing*; rob mclennan's above/ground press published a chapbook containing poems from "When a Folk, When a Sprawl;" and Klara du Plessis chose "I Am the Gold Machine" to be published in the "Poetic Systems" issue of Metatron's *Glyphöria.*

To the Montréal writing group who, as always, read it all first, thank you. William Vallières, Kasia van Schaik, Jessie Jones, Paige Cooper, and Sarah Burgoyne, your buoyant friendship makes the present possible.

To my family, I love you. Mom, Dad, Chelsea, Jake, and the rowdy kitchen of aunts, uncles, and cousins, for teaching me to live ferociously, thank you.

To Zac Abram, all of it. Love, thanks, desire. Always, eternally.